D1391735

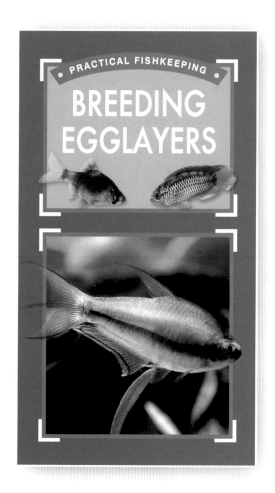

PRACTICAL FISHKEEPING

BREEDING EGGLAYERS

John Rundle

RINGPRESS

ABOUT THE AUTHOR

John Rundle, a former marine engineer, now devotes himself to breeding fish – a hobby he has enjoyed for more than 35 years. John writes for specialist fish and water-gardening magazines, and is a well-respected lecturer. He works part-time for the University of Plymouth, where he runs a breeding programme for cuttlefish at the Marine Biological Association of the UK.

SCIENTIFIC CONSULTANT: Dr. Peter Burgess BSc, MSc, MPhil, PhD is an experienced aquarium hobbyist and international consultant on ornamental fish.

Commercial products shown in this book are for illustrative purposes only and are not necessarily endorsed by the author.

Photography: John Rundle (p.5, p.9, p.28, p.33, p.34, p.52, p.58, p.59, p.63, p.64), Steve McMahon (p.27), Dr. David Ford (p.40), Dr. Peter Burgess (p.53), Mary Bailey (p.6), Keith Allison and courtesy of Tetra UK, and Interpet.
Line Drawings: Viv Rainsbury
Picture editor: Claire Horton-Bussey
Design: Rob Benson

Published by Ringpress Books,
a division of Interpet Publishing,
Vincent Lane, Dorking, Surrey, RH4 3YX, UK
Tel: 01306 873822 Fax: 01306 876712
email: sales@interpet.co.uk

First published 2002
© 2002 Ringpress Books. All rights reserved

ISBN 1 86054 266 2

Printed and bound in Hong Kong through
Printworks International Ltd.

10 9 8 7 6 5 4 3 2 1

CONTENTS

CHAPTER 1

INTRODUCTION

Some people ask why fishkeepers even bother to breed fish when they can buy all the fish they need from a dealer. The answer to this question can be summed up in a few key words:

- Knowledge
- Financial incentive
- Challenge
- Satisfaction
- Conservation.

GETTING HOOKED

To many fishkeepers, breeding fish is often the next step when they have mastered the basic principles of keeping them. Not only is it enjoyable and rewarding, it is also a means of gaining more knowledge of the hobby.

I was hooked on fish breeding more than 30 years ago by watching a female guppy give birth to her young in a community tank. I just had to know all about the strange and wonderful life cycle of this livebearing fish, and read all the books that could be found on the subject. The knowledge gained all that time ago about guppies stayed with me to this day. How many of you reading this book have gone through the guppy induction course? As your fish

There is no greater satisfaction than to see a fine shoal of young home-bred fish in your aquarium. Pictured: *Pseudochalceus kyburzi* tetras.

breeding experience grows, so will your knowledge. It could be water chemistry, fish nutrition or fish husbandry. Whatever it is, the education can only go to making you a better fishkeeper.

ABSORBING HOBBY

It should be emphasised that this book is aimed at the amateur hobbyist and not the professional fish breeder. Here the word 'amateur' is used for a person who breeds fish for a hobby not a profession. Even the term 'financial' is used loosely – it does not necessarily mean cash. There are dealers who will accept good-quality fish in exchange for new stock, food or equipment, so providing a financial saving for the fishkeeper. This applies both to the fish breeder with one or two tanks, or a large fish house. They both have to feed their fish.

CHALLENGE

The challenge factor when breeding fish is always present. It could be the challenge of successfully breeding and rearing your first ever brood of fish. Or, if you are more experienced, then that so-called 'problem' fish will throw down the gauntlet and challenge you to try to breed from it.

SATISFACTION

There is nothing more satisfying than showing a friend a shoal of fish in your community tank, which have been bred and raised by you.

CONSERVATION

There are many species of fish under threat in their own natural habitats. It could be that some of these species would not be considered worth importing for the

Some fish, including certain cichlid species, face an unknown future, and are reliant on specialist breeders in order to avoid extinction. Pictured: *Paretroplus maculatus*, a rare Madagascan cichlid.

ornamental trade, but that does not mean we should not be concerned about their plight or to do something about it by breeding them. There are specialist societies that keep and breed fish that are under threat, such as killifish, live-bearers, anabantids and cichlids.

There are many branches on the tree of fishkeeping, and breeding is only one of them. About 90 per cent of the fish we keep are captive-bred. So where would the hobby be if there were no fish breeders?

POPULAR SPECIES

It would be impossible to cover all the tropical egg-laying fish that can be bred by fishkeepers, so I have selected a variety of popular species and groups (see table below), and have discussed their need in Chapters 5 to 11. All of them can be readily obtained and are not difficult to breed.

The fish will be placed in groups according to their breeding strategies; however, it will be possible in some cases to use the same methods for other fish that have similar breeding habits.

GROUPS	SPECIES
TETRAS	Glowlight Tetra *Hemigrammus erythrozonus*
	Emperor Tetra *Nematobrycon palmeri*
BARBS	Tiger Barb *Puntius tetrazona*
DANIOS	Zebra Danio *Danio rerio*
LABYRINTHS	Pearl Gourami *Trichogaster leeri*
CATFISH	Peppered Catfish *Corydoras paleatus*
CICHLIDS	Golden Dwarf Cichlid *Nannacara anomala*

CHAPTER
2

GETTING STARTED

To get started, first, you need to obtain the fish that you will breed from. There are a few avenues that are open to you.

YOUNG STOCK FISH
Buying a group of about seven young fish is a good way to obtain brood stock. Do not buy small fry; your stockfish should be young adults. In fact, some of the tetra species are at their best for breeding when they are young adults.

In some cases, it may be possible to sex the fish you buy, but this is not a necessity, as the odds of having a mixed sex group are quite good.

COMMUNITY-TANK FISH
Even fish that are in the living-room community tank can be used for a breeding project. A key point when obtaining your breeding stock is to make sure that they are healthy and in good condition. Do not use fish that are deformed in any way or show signs of disease.

ADULT PAIR
It is possible to select and buy adult pairs of fish to use for a breeding project. I have often seen a pair of fish in a dealer's tank that are in breeding condition, and, without hesitation, have bought and bred them.

An adult pair of Black Phantom Tetas (*Hyphessobrycon megalopterus*) in breeding condition. They can often be found ready-matched in breeders' tanks.

ESSENTIAL EQUIPMENT

When breeding most of the popular species of freshwater tropical fish, it is not essential to have a large number of tanks or expensive filtration. The main difference between the fishkeeper breeding fish with just two or three tanks and the fishkeeper with a fish house that holds fifty tanks is the number of fish that each system can hold, and the number of species that can be bred at any one time.

One of the factors that govern the number of tanks is available space, but even a small space, such as an alcove of a room, may suffice for a breeding project.

TANK SIZES

Whatever fish you choose to breed, it is recommended that you have a minimum of two tanks: one for breeding and the other for growing on young fish. The size of the tanks required will be controlled by the species of fish being bred.

A range of average tank sizes that will cover all the fish in this book are in the table, page 10.

EXAMPLES OF STANDARD TANK SIZES		
LENGTH	DEPTH	WIDTH
30 cm (12 in)	20 cm (8 in)	20 cm (8 in)
61 cm (24 in)	30 cm (12 in)	30 cm (12 in)
91 cm (36 in)	30 cm (12 in)	30 cm (12 in)

Tank sizes quoted in this book are standard and can be obtained from aquarium shops. Use these sizes as a guide; tanks that vary slightly can still be used.

The correct size of tank required for the pair of fish should be selected. For example, it would not be practical to breed a pair of Neon Tetras in the size of tank required to breed an adult pair of Port Hoplo Catfish (*Megalechis thoracata*). The recommended sizes are explained in the relevant species sections (see Chapters 5 to 11).

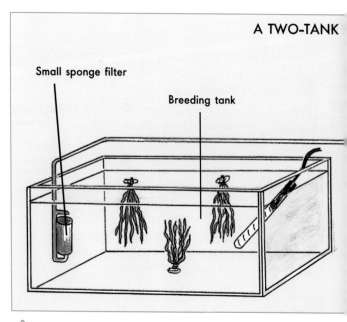

A TWO-TANK

Small sponge filter

Breeding tank

LIGHTING

In many cases, over-tank lighting is not necessary.
Normal daylight entering an area (room, shed or fish
house) through a window will be sufficient. If there are
no windows in the room, then the lights that are used
to illuminate these areas (e.g. room lamp) will supply
enough light to breed the fish. A portable light with a
long flex is ideal for examining the fry or young fish in
more detail.

FILTRATION

To breed the fish covered in this book and many other
species, there is no need to spend money on expensive
filtration systems. The filters recommended below are
basic, but effective and easy to maintain.

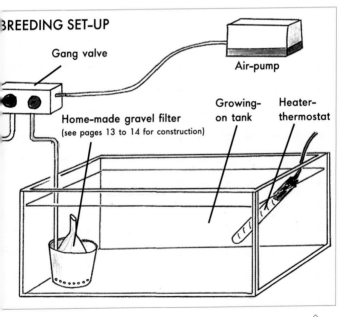

BREEDING SET-UP

Gang valve

Air-pump

Home-made gravel filter
(see pages 13 to 14 for construction)

Growing-
on tank

Heater-
thermostat

The size of breeding tank will be determined by the type of fish you use. A Neon Tetra (above) will need a much smaller aquarium than a large cat fish, such as the Port Hoplo Catfish (*Megalechis thoracata*) below.

SPONGE FILTERS

These act as a mechanical filter, meaning they remove particulate matter by passing water over or through a medium, such as a sponge. These filters also have a biological capacity (i.e. they contain bacteria that break down the fish's wastes). They can be bought as a complete unit from aquatic retailers.

They come in two sizes, one that suits small breeding tanks and the larger size that will filter a bigger breeding tank or even a growing-on tank.

Sponge filters have many advantages, including easy maintenance, and there is no danger of losing fry that are sucked into the filter.

BOX-TYPE FILTERS

These small plastic box-type internal filters have a mechanical and biological capacity. They have been used in the hobby for years, and can be found in any aquatic retail outlet. They can be used to hold various filter materials, such as synthetic wool and carbon. To stop any young fish becoming trapped within the filter, it is advisable to remove the filter box cover.

HOME-MADE FILTERS

These can be made to whatever size is required by the fishkeeper. For example, small ones for breeding tanks or a larger size to suit growing-on tanks.

These filters consist of three components:

- A plastic container, such as an ice-cream container.
- A plastic funnel.
- Aquarium gravel.

Around the base of the plastic container, make a series of holes about 3 mm ($1/8$ in) in diameter, then make another hole the diameter of a normal plastic aquarium airline.

Place enough aquarium gravel in the container to cover the 3 mm holes that are about 12 to 15 mm (about $1/2$ in) up from the base.

A HOME-MADE FILTER

There is no limit for the size of these filters

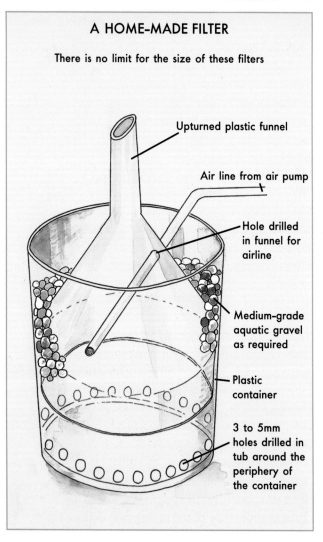

Upturned plastic funnel

Air line from air pump

Hole drilled in funnel for airline

Medium-grade aquatic gravel as required

Plastic container

3 to 5mm holes drilled in tub around the periphery of the container

Rest the funnel on top of the gravel, and then continue to fill up the container with more gravel. Every time you carry out a water change, just clean the filter gravel in old tank water and then replace it back in the filter.

AIR SUPPLY

All of these filters require the use of air to work, which is supplied by an electric air pump. Often, fishkeepers try to supply a bank of tanks with a pump that has too small a capacity. It is far better to buy a pump with more capacity than is required; this will ensure that all the tanks have an adequate air supply.

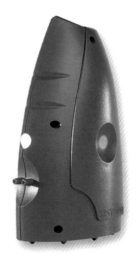

The filter needs to be powered by an electric air pump, shown above.

HEATING

All the fish in this book will require the water in their tanks to be within a temperature range of between 24°C to 28°C (75°F to 82°F). This can be achieved by using individual combined heater/thermostats or by heating the space around the tanks. Space-heating is often found in fish houses where a large number of tanks are held. For novice breeders, ordinary heater/thermostats should be sufficient.

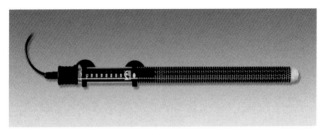

A stable water temperature is maintained in the tank via an electric heater-thermostat.

> **WATER**
> Water quality is a very important factor when breeding aquarium fish. With each fish-breeding project covered in this book, a set of water-quality parameters (pH and dH) are suggested.

WATER TEST KITS

Water conditions can be a controlling factor on whether fish will breed, and tap water can vary in different areas. For this reason, it is recommended that the water be tested for pH and hardness.

Test kits based on a simple colour change can be obtained from aquarium shops.

pH

The pH is a measure of the degree of acidity or alkalinity of aquarium water. pH is measured on a scale 0 to 14. A pH of 7 indicates the water is neutral. Below 7 means the water is acidic, and above 7 indicates that the water is alkaline.

HARDNESS

Hardness is the measure of the amount of dissolved salts (principally of calcium or magnesium) in the water. dH is measured in degrees of German (total) hardness (^{o}dH). See box, below.

In general terms, water hardness is classed as:

0 - 4 dH	Very soft
4 - 8 dH	Soft
8 - 12 dH	Medium hard
12 - 18 dH	Fairly hard
18 - 30 dH	Hard.

SPAWNING MOPS

Nylon wool spawning mops are useful in certain breeding tank set-ups, and the fish will deposit their eggs on them. The mops also provide cover and security for the newborn fry. They can be suspended on cork or a strip of polystyrene in the tank. Alternatively, you can fix them to the bottom of the tank, rooted in the substrate.

1 Wrap nylon wool around a block of wood around 15 cm (6 in) in length, and cut through with a sharp knife. Tip: to fool the fish into thinking the mops are plants, choose green wool!

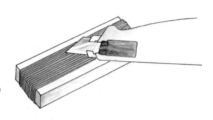

2 Tie a piece of wool around the middle of the strands.

3 Create a loop at the top of the strands and then secure the knot. Trim any loose ends where necessary.

CHAPTER

3

TANK SET-UPS

It is possible for tropical egg-laying aquarium fish to breed within the confines of a community tank. However, this situation is not practical if the fishkeeper wishes to keep and raise any of the progeny from these random, uncontrolled spawnings. For example, tetras, barbs and danios will scatter their eggs. But not many will survive, if any at all. What will probably happen is that the other tank inmates will devour the eggs. The

A general community aquarium is not suitable for a breeding project – separate tanks must be used. This well-established community aquarium contains Harlequin Rasboras and Rummy-nose Tetras.

fry too will be preyed upon and any survivors may struggle to obtain food of the correct quality and quantity in the community tank.

The key to successful fish breeding is 'control': the fishkeeper has to control the conditions, and, in some cases, the timing of spawnings, and must also control the conditions for rearing the fry.

The main part of this control makes it necessary to have special breeding set-ups and methods based on the fishes' natural breeding strategies. It will be noted that some of the breeding tank set-ups described in this book are quite sparse, while others will be based on typical planted systems.

To look at this in more detail, it is necessary to consider the way fish live and breed in their own natural biotopes. In the wild, they have access to:

- **Space:** most types of fish have the space of a large pond, stream or even a river. Here, they can breed using all the room they require.

- **Water:** they will, of course, have the correct natural water chemistry to live and breed in.

- **Filtration:** a fair percentage of fish will live in waters that have movement. This natural flow serves as a very superior filter with its regular water changes. Water movement assists in keeping eggs clean and bears small food particles for the newborn fry.

- **Food:** the water flow can carry a source of food. A good example of this is the thousands of Cardinal Tetras that spawn in the Amazonian rainy season.

In the wild, Cardinal Tetras spawn to coincide with the Amazon rainy season, which brings an abundance of food.

They instinctively know that, when the rivers flood, there will be food of the correct type and it will be in ample supply to feed the fry.

- **Natural culling:** a great number of species are very prolific and produce many offspring. The reason for this is that many of the eggs and newborn fry can become a meal for predators. This, in many ways, can be a natural culling system, allowing good-quality fish to survive.

FURNISHED OR BARE?

There will be two basic set-ups used for breeding the fish in this book: the furnished tank and the bare tank.

THE FURNISHED TANK

This set-up consists of gravel, plants, and rockwork; in fact, it is similar to a community tank. The difference will be that it will typically hold just one or two pairs of the fish that you want to breed. This will certainly avoid the problem of other tank inmates eating the eggs or fry.

THE BARE TANK

This set-up is called a 'bare tank' because it has no substrate (gravel) on the tank base. Most of the fish discussed in this book are bred in sparse set-ups. Fish that can be successfully bred in this set-up are tetras, barbs, danios, rasboras, gouramis and catfish.

With this type of set-up you have control over:

- **Tank cleanliness:** this is a main factor when breeding fish. A bare tank can be thoroughly cleaned prior to the spawning, and also enables easy removal of debris from the tank floor when the fish have bred.

- **Ability to save eggs or fry:** when breeding fish that are avid egg-eaters, mesh grids can be fitted to let the eggs pass through on to the tank base out of harm's way. This allows the fish breeder to save most of the eggs, and to raise a decent size brood.

A bare tank set-up is ideal for breeding many fish, including the Dwarf Gourami (*Colisa lalia*) pictured.

- **Feeding:** the bare tank is an asset when feeding fry, as it allows the fishkeeper easily to see the amount of uneaten food. Live foods and dry foods can, if overfed, lead to pollution and the subsequent death of any fry. The bare tank will allow any uneaten food to be removed with ease, by means of a small water change (e.g. using a small-bore siphon tube).

- **Observation:** the need to observe clearly all the activities in the breeding tank is a key factor when breeding fish. You want to see when the fish spawn, the development of the eggs, and the fry when they hatch.

SPAWNING GRID MADE FROM PLASTIC NETTING

A spawning grid, slightly raised from the bottom of the tank, will allow eggs to pass through so that they are out of reach of the other fish.

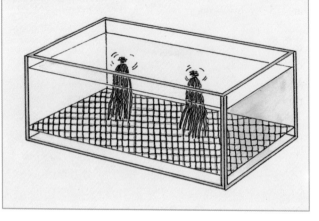

CHAPTER
4

CONDITIONING FISH FOR BREEDING

Before fish will breed, there are certain factors (such as a change of water and temperature, or an abundance of food) that have to be in place. All these factors work towards bringing the fish into breeding condition, followed by them actually spawning.

A good example of this is the many Amazonian fish that will only breed when the rainy season starts and the river floods. Here, we have natural changes in water, temperature and an abundance of live food (such as fly larvae and tiny freshwater shrimps) for the parents and resulting fry. See *Live Foods for Freshwater Fishes* in this *Practical Fishkeeping* series.

About 90 per cent of the fish available to fishkeepers are captive-bred, the other 10 per cent being collected from the wild. This means that there is a good chance that the fish you intend to breed have never been near their natural home. The bulk of these captive-bred fish are the popular aquarium species that we will look at in this book.

Among the species of the 10 per cent of wild-collected fish are the 'problem fish', so called because they are difficult to breed or have never been bred under aquarium conditions. The reasons for this may be because the 'breeding conditioning' factors have not yet been achieved or elucidated by fishkeepers.

THINNING OUT

It will be seen that all the fish mentioned in the breeding projects can have quite large broods, and this could be a problem if space is limited. Do not attempt to raise more fish than a system (tank or tanks) will safely contain. Fish kept in overcrowded conditions will stunt growth rates, cause deformities and produce runts. It will also leave the system wide open for disease problems.

If space is a problem, then the brood will have to be thinned out by 'culling' out any runts or deformed fish. It may also be necessary to remove good-quality fish to reach a safe number that the system will hold. Only raise enough fish from the brood that you have room for. It is better to raise 50 healthy fish than 200 runts.

Runts and deformed fish should always be destroyed. Provided they show no sign of disease, they can be fed to larger fish, which is what would happen if they hatched in the wild. If you have good, healthy surplus stock, perhaps you can pass them on to fishkeeping friends.

'Problem fish' are difficult to breed, and are usually collected from the wild. Pictured: Chocolate Gourami, a fish that has rarely been bred in captivity.

CHAPTER
5

GLOWLIGHT TETRA

The Glowlight Tetra, *Hemigrammus erythrozonus*, is a popular, small, peaceful schooling fish.

SEX DIFFERENCES
The Glowlight can be sexed by body shape. Males are slim, and the females are larger and more robust in the belly region. When in breeding condition, the females will be quite fat.

BREEDING TANK SET-UP
A large tank is not required: use a tank with the dimensions 46 x 25 x 25 cm (18 x 12 x 12 in), based on the 'bare tank' set-up (page 21) with just a heater/stat, spawning medium, and filter (see page 32 for the set-up illustration.)

The Glowlight Tetra is a popular, attractive, egglaying fish.

Try not to exceed water parameters of 7.2 pH and 6.5° dH, and set the temperature between 25°C to 26°C (77°F to 79°F).

FILTRATION

A small sponge filter is all that is required. However, do not fit it until the eggs are laid and the parents are removed. Up to this point, just have an open-ended airline in the tank with not too fierce an airflow.

SPAWNING MEDIUM

Use home-made spawning mops, made from green nylon wool (see diagram, page 17). Float one mop, suspended on a cork or strip of polystyrene, in the tank. Then place directly under this mop two more mops that will rest on the base of the tank. Make sure the mops are clean by washing them in hot water before they are used.

The Glowlight is a prolific egglayer, producing around 200 eggs. Pictured: female in breeding condition.

SPAWNING

The selected pair of conditioned fish should be placed in the tank in the evening and normally start their spawning dance in the early morning. The male, in his best colours, dances around the female and will drive her in and over the spawning mops. The pair lock fins quickly, embrace and do a barrel roll while a few slightly adhesive eggs are extruded and fertilised. This all takes place using only a small area of the tank – in fact, just in and around the vicinity of the mops.

CARE OF THE EGGS

The Glowlight is a prolific egg-layer with around 200 eggs being laid by an adult pair. The spawning procedure can take up to two hours.

An indication that spawning is complete is when the female hides from the male and shows signs of being slimmer. It is now time to remove both parents; if they are left in the tank, they will eat the eggs. Now fit the sponge filter, and cover the tank with newspaper to keep it in semi-darkness, as the eggs of most tetras can be sensitive to strong light.

EGG HATCHING TIME

Within 24 to 36 hours, the eggs will hatch, and, if the mops are gently lifted, very tiny wriggling yolk-sac larvae will be seen on the base of the tank.

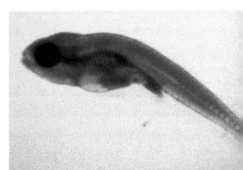

Yolk-sac larvae will be seen in the mops after 24 to 36 hours. Pictured: a tetra fry, measuring just 2 mm in length.

FEEDING THE FRY

The fry will feed on their yolk-sac for about five days,
and at this stage they will become free-swimming. It
must be stressed that no food must be placed in the
tank until the fry can swim of their own accord. The fry
are very tiny and will require a minute first food and
plenty of it. A fry feeding menu would be:

- **First food**: cultured infusoria (see *Live Foods for
  Aquarium Fishes*, Ringpress Books). About 200 ml of
  good-quality culture will feed 150 Glowlight fry.
  They will feed on this food for about four to five
  days before moving on to second foods.
- **Second foods**: Brine shrimp nauplii and microworm.
  (Again, see *Live Foods For Aquarium Fishes*.)

A cloud of
infusoria – a
good first food
for tetra fry.

Care must be taken not to overfeed. Only feed enough of these foods according to the size of the brood. If the brood is overfed, instantly remove all the live food that dies.

WATER CHANGES

Carry out a 25 per cent water change once a week, and make sure that the replaced water has the same pH and hardness. Take away any uneaten food, and be careful not to remove the fry in the process.

GROWING ON

A reduction in numbers from the eggs hatching to the free-swimming stage is not unusual. On average, 150 fish can be raised to adults. The growth rate for the Glowlight is fairly constant, and, when they are about 3 to 4 mm ($^1/_8$ in), they will require moving to a larger tank by using a small fine-mesh net. At this time, they will be able to take dry fry foods and live grindalworm (for further information, see *Live Foods for Aquarium Fishes* in this *Practical Fishkeeping* series).

With experience and care, around 150 Glowlight Tetra fry can be raised to adulthood. Pictured: adult female Glowlight Tetra.

CHAPTER
6

EMPEROR TETRA

Since its first introduction to the hobby in 1959, *Nematobrycon palmeri* has maintained its popularity on two fronts – its peaceful manner and its very attractive coloration. Both of these factors make it an ideal community tank fish; add to this that it is easy to breed if given the right conditions, and you have a fishkeeper's dream.

The early literature on *N. palmeri* suggests that it can be kept in very soft water and an acid pH, as the early imports were only one or two generations from the wild stock. Nowadays, the Emperor Tetras that we see in dealers' tanks are from either local breeders or

The Emperor Tetra is an attractive, peaceful fish that does well in a community aquarium.

commercial farms, and, as such, are more accustomed to some variations in water quality. Nevertheless, they still do not take to hard water.

SEXING

It is the male that carries the distinctive features of sexual dimorphism (i.e. the sexual characteristics that differentiate the sexes); he has fairly long extensions to the central rays of the caudal fins. When the fish are young and the males not yet showing the tail extensions, look at their eyes – the males have a bright blue iris; in females, it is yellow. Females tend to be smaller and more robust than the male when full grown.

BREEDING

The Emperor Tetra spawns readily and the fry should not be a problem to feed and raise. However, a key factor, which must be considered, is the age of the intended breeding pairs. It is best to use young adult Emperors, which will spawn readily and supply between 50 to 150 eggs. Emperors are not known for producing the large number of eggs that some other tetras can produce.

BREEDING TANK SET-UP

Emperors do not require a large tank to spawn in. Use a tank that is 46 x 20 x 20 cm (18 x 8 x 8 in), filled to a depth of 15 cm (6 in). Ensure that the tank is thoroughly cleaned prior to filling with water. Ideally, the water should have a pH of 6.5 to 7.2 and with a hardness of not higher than 6° dH. However, they will breed in water with a pH that's a little higher and moderately soft.

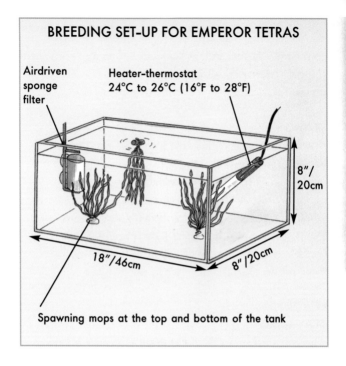

BREEDING SET-UP FOR EMPEROR TETRAS

Airdriven sponge filter

Heater-thermostat
24°C to 26°C (16°F to 28°F)

8" / 20cm

18"/46cm

8" /20cm

Spawning mops at the top and bottom of the tank

The set-up is of the 'bare tank' mode, that is to say no substrate. The only items in the tank are wool spawning mops – two resting on the base of the tank and one suspended on a cork. Along with the mops is an open-ended airline with a slow flow of bubbles.

Do not fit a filter at this stage. A temperature of between 24°C to 26°C (76°F to 78°F) is fine for this project.

SELECTING A PAIR

The point of using young adults for breeding stock has already been mentioned. It is also worth noting that Emperor females do not have to be all that plump to breed. This could be because of the small numbers of eggs that are released.

The male will drive the female into the mops for the eggs to be laid. Pictured: a spawning pair of Emperor Tetras.

SPAWNING

The pair of fish is placed in the tank in the evening to give the fish a chance to become acclimatised to the breeding tank. The majority of pairs will spawn on the second morning. The male, in his best colours, will chase and drive the female into the mops and here the tiny eggs are laid. You will not see many eggs outside the mop area; they tend to be hidden within.

Spawning can be a lengthy affair, taking up to four hours. After spawning is over, the parents should be removed, as they will soon eat the eggs if left in the tank. It is at this stage that you should fit a small sponge filter.

RAISING THE FRY

At 26°C (78°F) the eggs hatch within 30 hours. The yolk-sac larvae will stay hidden in the confines of the mops, and, if one is gently lifted (do not do this too often), they will be seen like very tiny splinters falling to the tank floor. They will not look like fish, just a clear wriggling head and tail, and, of course, a yolk-sac.

The larvae will feed off this yolk-sac for about five days, so do not attempt to feed them. When the yolk-sac is absorbed, the larvae will be seen free-swimming, and it is at this point that they will need to be fed. Even at this stage, they tend to seek somewhere to hide, so leave just one suspended mop in the tank until they venture into open water.

- **First food**: use infusoria, which they will feed on for about ten days. Now and then, drop a few brine shrimp nauplii into the tank. If the fry take it, you will know that they are ready for their next food.
- **Second foods**: a good diet of second foods is brine shrimp nauplii in the morning and microworm in the evening. Once on these foods, growth is fast.

When the fry is 25 mm in length, the fry can join the adult fish.

A group of young Emperor Tetras at 12 weeks of age (about 30mm in length).

GROWING ON

When the fry are about 3 mm (^{1}/$_8$ in), move them on to a larger growing-on tank. At the age of 8 weeks, you should have young fish of 20 mm to 25 mm (1 in) in length, and the males will start to get their central tail spike. At 25 mm the fish are large enough to go into a tank with other fish.

CHAPTER 7

TIGER BARB

The Tiger Barb *(Puntius tetrazona)* has the reputation of being a fin nipper. This is often the case when kept as a solitary fish in a community-tank situation. But when kept in a shoal, these striking fish tend to lose the habit of nipping other tankmates' fins. Besides being a colourful fish, the Tiger Barb makes an ideal project for a novice fish breeder.

The fin-nipping Tiger Barb lives up to its predatory name!

The Tiger Barb usually requires a well-decorated tank, but a bare set-up should be used for breeding projects.

SEX DIFFERENCES

There will not be a problem when choosing a pair of these fish to breed. When in breeding condition the female takes on a very robust look and is fat in the belly region. The male is quite slender when compared to the female, and will also show more colour in areas such as the fins when in breeding condition. Adults can be up to 7 cm (2.8 in) in length, but the fish will breed before they reach this size.

BREEDING SET-UP

Like most of the barbs, the Tiger Barb can be prolific when breeding, laying 200-plus eggs. Also, the males will chase the females over the full area of the breeding tank (not like the more confined spawning area of the tetras). For these reasons, a 60 x 30 x 30 cm (24 x 12 x 12 in) breeding tank is recommended.

The set-up is based on the bare-tank method as follows:

- **Water conditions**: try not to exceed a pH of 7.2 and 6 dH.
- **Temperature**: 25°C to 26°C (77°F to 78°F).
- **Filtration**: a sponge filter is ideal. But do not fit it until the eggs are laid and the parents are removed. Just have an open-ended airline with not-too-fast an airflow in the tank up to the point that the fish spawn.

The Tiger Barb comes in several colour varieties and this must be a consideration when planning a breeding programme.
Pictured: green (above) and gold (below) types.

- **Spawning medium**: wool mops are used, and, because of the area covered when spawning and the dispersal of the barbs' adhesive eggs, it is necessary to use two to three floating mops and three mops on the tank base.

BREEDING METHOD

Place the selected pair of fish into the breeding tank in the evening, making sure that the female is showing the characteristic signs of carrying eggs and being ready to spawn. If this is the case, the male will start to chase the female the next morning. At intervals during the chase, the male will drive the female into the mops. Both fish will come together momentarily and the tiny sticky eggs will be released and fertilised. This can go on for a period of up to two hours.

Once the male loses interest and the female is spent of her eggs, they must be removed from the tank before they both start to eat their eggs. At this point, fit the sponge filter. The eggs are not as sensitive to light as the tetras, so there is no need to cover the tank. The eggs, which could exceed 200 in number, hatch in about 32 hours.

FRY CARE

For another four to five days, the larvae will feed on their yolk-sacs. It is only when they are seen free-swimming that they must be fed.

- **First food**: as a rule, this first feed will be infusoria. Broods of Tiger Barb fry have been known to take newly-hatched brine shrimp as a first food.
- **Second foods**: brine shrimp and microworm.

Warning: like most barbs, the fry and young of Tiger Barbs are prone to attacks of velvet disease (*Piscinoodnium*). This can be kept at bay by good husbandry techniques. (For more information on this, and other diseases, see *A-Z of Tropical Fish Diseases and Health Problems* by Peter Burgess, published by Ringpress Books.)

Tiger Barb fry will often take brine shrimp as a first food. Picture: Culture of brine shrimp.

Take care how much brine shrimp is placed in the tank at feeding time, and remove any uneaten dead brine shrimp. Carry out water changes of 25 per cent each week.

GROWING ON

When the young fish are about 3 to 4 mm ($1/8$ in), split the brood into other tanks. At this size, they take crushed flake foods and will be starting to show their tiger stripes.

CHAPTER

8

ZEBRA DANIO

I would place the Zebra Danio (*Danio rerio*) in the top ten of favourite community fish.

The Zebra Danio's natural home is India, and it was first introduced to the hobby in 1905. It soon became popular with fishkeepers worldwide because of its small size (reaching 6 cm/2.5 in), striking colours and pattern, and its peaceful nature.

The Zebra Danio was also found to be a prolific spawner. Producing up to 400 fry per brood, it is not surprising that the Zebra Danio became a very popular fish with commercial fish breeders too.

The Zebra Danio, a prolific spawner, is an ideal fish for the first-time hobbyist breeder.

BREEDING

Selecting a male and female is not a difficult task – the male is smaller and slimmer, whereas the female (when in breeding condition) is rotund in the belly region and tends to be slightly larger than the male. Try to choose fish that have good colour patterns for breeding.

This is a fish that can be found in dealers' tanks throughout the world, thus making it adaptable to various water chemistries. This allows a fair tolerance when it comes to breeding. The ideal water conditions would be around neutral pH (pH 7.0) and up to 12dH.

TANK SET-UP

Although Zebra Danios will spawn in a very small tank, bear in mind the large number of eggs and fry. Hence, the minimum tank size should be 46 x 20 x 20 cm (18 x 8 x 8 in).

These fish will devour their own eggs if given the chance, even to the point of eating them before they reach the tank bottom! There are various ways to ease this problem – use a shallow tank, or, in deeper tanks, keep the water level down. To protect the eggs (which are non-adhesive), a spawning grid can be used. Alternatively, as is the traditional method, the tank base can be covered in glass marbles.

The following recommended method is based on using just a shallow water depth of about 150 mm (6 in), and suspending spawning mops as well as placing them on the tank bottom. This will still supply enough eggs and fry to contend with. Filtration is supplied by a sponge-type filter, but do not fit it before the eggs are laid; just have an open-ended airline in the tank. The temperature is set to 25°C (77°F).

THREE METHODS FOR
BREEDING ZEBRA DANIOS

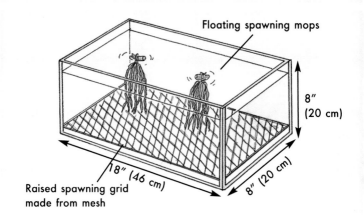

Floating spawning mops

8"
(20 cm)

18" (46 cm)

8" (20 cm)

Raised spawning grid
made from mesh

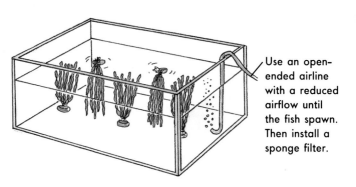

Use an open-
ended airline
with a reduced
airflow until
the fish spawn.
Then install a
sponge filter.

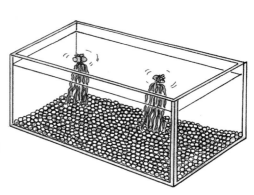

A single layer
of glass
marbles can
also be used
on the base of
the tank.

Zebra Danios, in common with other danios, usually spawn in the
early morning.

BREEDING PROCEDURE

The selected pair of fish is placed in the tank in the
evening, and, if the female is in condition, the
spawning procedure will usually take place the next day.
Like most of the danios, early morning daylight and the
new water seem to be a trigger for them to start
spawning. Both fish are very active when breeding, and
cover the whole area of the tank, with the male chasing
the female and driving her over and into the mops.
Here, the pair will embrace and scatter some eggs that
are instantly fertilised. This action will go on until the
female is void of eggs. Make sure the parents are
removed as soon as possible after the spawning and
then fit a sponge filter.

REARING THE FRY

The tiny clear eggs will hatch after about 36 hours, and
the larvae will be seen hanging on the tank sides and
also suspended from the strands of the mops. They
appear splinter-like and are dark in colour, and will
continue feeding off their yolk-sac for five or six days.

After this, they should be at the free-swimming stage, at which point they should be supplied with food.

- **First food:** the tiny fry will require a good-quality infusoria as their first food and it must be in a quantity where the fry do not have to hunt for it.
- **Second foods:** it can be up to seven days from free-swimming when the fry are large enough to take brine shrimp nauplii. It all depends on the quality and how much infusoria is available

Once on brine shrimp, and coupled with weekly 25 per cent water changes, the fry will soon grow. If all has gone to plan, you could have anything from 200 to 400 fry, so you must think of splitting the brood into two or more batches.

If you do not have the extra tanks, then you should think about culling some of the brood. Do not try to raise a large number of fish in a small breeding tank – it is far better to raise 40 good fish than 200 runts.

A PROBLEM
It is possible to buy a pair of Zebra Danios that, for all intents and purposes, look like normal short-finned fish. However, when they are eventually bred, and the fry begin to grow, it can become apparent that all is not as it should be. Instead of 100 per cent normal-finned Zebra Danios, there could be a mixture of three types of fish in the brood:

- Short-finned
- Long-finned
- Leopard-patterned.

The latter type of fish, sold under the common name of the Leopard Danio, has been the subject of much debate as to its validity as a true species. The problem seems to lie with the commercial breeders who have at some time allowed the various varieties to cross-breed. The result of all this is that it makes it hard for anyone in the hobby wishing to breed the Zebra Danio, taking a fair amount of work to return to the original fish.

So where do we go from here? I can only suggest that, first, you should decide what you want to breed – that is to say, either the normal short-finned type or the long-finned type. Then search dealers' tanks for set-ups that only contain your chosen fish.

Also make sure that there are no signs of any leopard pattern. You could still end up with non-pure stock, but you have to start somewhere.

Breeding stock must be kept pure, so it is important to keep the Zebra Danio varieties separate. Pictured: a leopard-patterned fish.

CHAPTER
9

PEARL GOURAMI

This fish has the Latin name of *Trichogaster leeri*, but can be found in aquarium shop tanks under one of three common names:

- Mosaic Gourami
- Lace Gourami
- Pearl Gourami.

This beautiful gourami fish has all the requirements of a perfect ornamental aquarium fish – not only is it colourful, but it also makes a good community tankmate. For the would-be breeder, the Pearl Gourami is ideal for a first-time gourami project.

The Pearl Gourami: attractive, colourful, and an ideal community tankmate.

COLOUR AND SEXING

It is the colours of these fish that make it so popular with fishkeepers. Even when it comes down to defining the sexes, colour is still a factor, along with fins and body shape.

An adult male will have a longer and more pointed dorsal fin and anal fin. Also, these fins will have extended rays that take the appearance of a lacy fringe (hence the name Lace Gourami). At times, it can look as though these fins are ragged and torn, but this is natural. The male should also have a beautiful reddish-orange colour spreading from its chin down into its breast.

The female's dorsal and anal fins are rounded at the extremities, and her belly region is somewhat rotund. She will also lack the reddish-orange colour of the male.

BREEDING

Using a full-grown (12 cm/5 in) pair of Pearl Gouramis, up to 1,000 eggs are not unusual. So it soon becomes obvious that tank sizes are an important factor.

TANK SET-UP

This fish can yield many eggs and fry, so use a 90 x 30 x 30 cm (36 x 12 x 12 in) tank for breeding; if the brood is a large one, it would have to be split into other tanks as the fish grow. If you only have one tank, then you must cull and only raise the amount of fry that the tank will hold without being overcrowded.

There are fishkeepers who breed species of gouramies such as the Pearl with success in a tank set-up with gravel and plants. However, the bare tank set-up, having no substrate, will allow more control for the fish breeder. The tank will have a sponge-type filter and plants such as Java Fern (*Microsorium pteropus*) and Java Moss (*Vesicularia dubyana*) placed on the tank base, and young Indian Fern (*Ceratopteris*) plants floating on the surface. The temperature can be between 26-28°C (78-82°F).

Water chemistry for this fish should not be too much of a problem; this can be noted by the fact it can be found in dealers' tanks throughout the country. The parameters to aim for are a pH between 6.6 and 7.6, and hardness should be moderately soft to moderately hard. Avoid extremes or sudden changes in water conditions.

Plants such as Java Fern (pictured) can be used in a Pearl Gourami breeding tank.

BREEDING PROCEDURE

The Pearl Gourami is generally classed as a bubble-nester, manufacturing a floating nest of air bubbles to hold its eggs (see below). It is a fish that should not give too many problems for the fish breeder. However, there are a few ground rules that should be observed.

It is imperative that the selected pair of fish is first ready to breed. It is possible to have a situation where the female Pearl Gourami is in condition, her belly

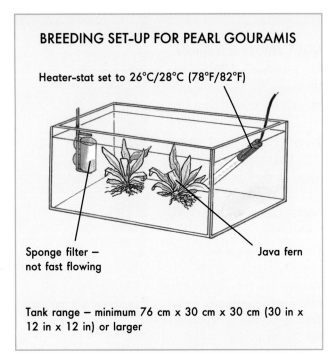

BREEDING SET-UP FOR PEARL GOURAMIS

Heater-stat set to 26°C/28°C (78°F/82°F)

Sponge filter –
not fast flowing

Java fern

Tank range – minimum 76 cm x 30 cm x 30 cm (30 in x
12 in x 12 in) or larger

region swollen with eggs. But when the pair is put
together, the male is just interested in chasing the
female relentlessly around the tank, with no intention
of blowing a bubble-nest.

Here is one way to overcome such a problem. Keep a
ratio of one male to two females (it could be two males
to four females). These fish would be held in a stock or
community tank with other fish. Here, they are
conditioned and each male is allowed to select a partner
of his choice. Once he shows signs of willingness to
breed and not just total aggression, remove the pair to
the breeding tank.

It is, of course, possible that you could buy just one
pair, that they will breed, and that the male will be a
good father.

COURTSHIP AND MATING

Once a selected pair has been placed in the breeding tank, the courtship ritual will begin by the male displaying all his best colours and outstretched fins to the female. Some chasing follows, and then the male will attempt to draw the female to his selected breeding area. Here, the male will start to construct a bubble-nest at the surface, made up of small mucus-coated bubbles that will hold and support the eggs. The completed bubble-nest will have a fairly large surface area several centimetres across.

Once the nest-building is complete, the intensity of the courtship increases, until the female ends up under the canopy of the nest. It is at this point that the pair will lock together in an embrace. During this clinch, the buoyant eggs released from the female and fertilised by the male will rise towards the surface and the bubble-nest. When contact is broken between the pair of fish, the female will often head for cover, while the male collects any loose eggs in his mouth and places them in the nest.

This procedure will continue with further embraces, sending about 40 to 70 eggs to the bubble-nest each time, until the female is spent. Once spawning is complete, the male will drive the female away from the nest site, and he will stand guard and work to keep the bubble-nest in good repair and stop any eggs breaking free from it.

Remove the female at this stage and make sure that there is not too much water surface movement that would otherwise disturb the bubble-nest.

Nests will begin to disintegrate if the temperature is too high, so keep the tank between the limits outlined for breeding: 26°C to 28°C (78°F to 82°F).

RAISING THE FRY

At the higher end of the recommended temperature range, the eggs will hatch in just over 24 hours. The fry appear as very tiny splinters, appearing as just a head and a tail, some of which will be seen at times falling from the nest. The male will retrieve these strays and spit them back into the protection of the bubbles.

Within three days, the fry will be free-swimming and ready for food (until now they have fed off their own yolk-sac). During this period, the male can become a little bit agitated, tending the nest and the now-active fry. Males can get frustrated from trying to catch the fry and replace them back into a nest that, by this time, may be starting to deflate and break up. When in this state, he could eat the brood. So when the brood is in free-swimming mode, remove the male back to the stock tank.

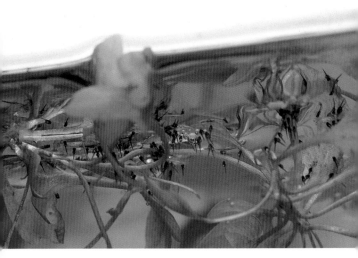

Gourami yolk-sac larvae at the surface of the water. At this stage, they should not be fed.

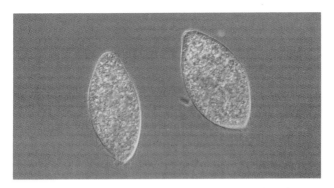

Infusoria (pictured at high magnification) is an ideal first food for new Gourami fry.

The critical point in breeding Pearl Gouramies comes now, for there could be a large brood of fry (up to 1,000) and they are very tiny. So there must be large amounts of food that is minute in size. It is often the failure to meet these food requirements that can cause the bulk of the brood to die through starvation.

- **First food**: to meet the first food criterion use cultured infusoria until the brood can take larger food.
- **Second foods**: in about six days, the fry should be of a size that will be able to take brine shrimp nauplii as their next food. Once on this food, growth is fast and regular partial water changes (25 per cent, twice weekly) will now help to maintain water quality.

GROWING ON AND SORTING

Gourami fry tend to have a varying growth rate. This means that the larger, more dominant, young fish will obtain the bulk of the food at feeding time. So it is wise to sort the brood to allow smaller fish to get their share of food and grow.

Extra tanks are required to accommodate fish, such as the Pearl Gourami, that have large broods. If space is limited, only raise the amount of fish that you can accommodate and grow on. This is much more preferable to trying to raise the full brood in cramped conditions and subsequently ending up with poor stock.

When the fry are about 3 mm ($^1/8$ in) long they will take very fine flake foods, and, when about 6 weeks old, the largest should be about 20 mm ($^3/4$ in) long. At six weeks, they will be showing the body markings of the adults and will be well on the way to obtaining the beauty of the Pearl Gourami.

CORYDORAS PALEATUS

There are more than 100 species of the small South American mailed catfish in the genus *Corydoras*. One of the most popular must be the Peppered Catfish (*Corydoras paleatus*). A peaceful nature, an attractive body colour, and an adult size of 7 cm (2 $^3/_4$ in) are a few of the reasons for its popularity.

The key to breeding fish from this genus is being able to trigger conditioned pairs to spawn. Fortunately, the Peppered Catfish tends to be a species that is not too difficult to encourage to breed.

The Peppered Catfish (*Corydoras paleatus*) is one of the more popular species, and is relatively easy to breed.

CORYDORAS VARIETIES
There are more than 100 species of Corydoras catfish

▲ *Corydoras trilineatus.*

▲ *Corydoras aeneus.*

▲ *Corydoras cf. melanistius.*

CONDITIONING FOR BREEDING

Species of *Corydoras* are often bought by fishkeepers as
'scavengers' and virtually left to feed on scraps not eaten
by other tankmates. On this scant diet, the chances of the
fish coming into breeding condition are low.

The catfish must be fed the same top-quality foods as
any other type of fish. On the following diet, they should
come into breeding condition.

- Dry foods, such as flake, sinking tablets
- Frozen foods, such as bloodworm
- Live foods, such as grindalworm, whiteworm,
  daphnia and bloodworm.

SEXING

The males of the Peppered Catfish are somewhat smaller
than the females, and their pectoral fins are more
pointed. Females are deeper and rounded in body shape
(see photo overleaf). When the female is in breeding
condition, her very rotund belly will leave the fishkeeper
in no doubt that she is carrying eggs.

BREEDING TANK SET-UP

Tanks within the range of 45 x 25 x 25 cm (18 x 10 x 10
in) to 60 x 30 x 30 cm (24 x 12 x 12 in) can be used. It
is recommended that groups of fish (a minimum of 6) be
used with a ratio of two males to one female.

Plants such as Java Fern (*Microsorium pteropus*) should
be placed in the tank. For filtration, use a sponge filter.
The choice of set-up is up to you – these fish will spawn
with or without gravel.

Water conditions should be pH 6.5 to 7 and up to 12°
dH, and the temperature should be set to 24°C (75°F).

THE 'T-POSITION'

A large female *Corydoras paleatus* with one of the males near her mouth region in the mating T-position.

A close-up of the T-position with the male on the right. This can last up to 15 seconds.

BREEDING METHOD

Assuming the fish are in breeding condition, they can be triggered to spawn simply by a normal partial water change, or with water that is cool enough to gradually lower the temperature to 18°C (65°F) and allowing it to warm to normal temperature. Signs of breeding activity are the males chasing the females and both sexes cleaning the tank sides or the leaves of the plants

The female deposits her sticky eggs on to the side of the tank.

(they seem to require very clean sites to deposit their eggs).

When the spawning sequence starts, the female will take up the now well-recorded 'T' position. In this, the male will position himself in front of the female who will nudge his side and then place her mouth over the male's vent. They can stay locked in the position for up to 15 seconds, during which sperm is passed into the female's mouth.

When they break apart, the female will be seen with about five eggs clasped between her pelvic fins. She then swims and looks for an egg deposition site – this could be by the sides of the tank, among plant leaves or even in the sponge filter. Here, the sticky eggs are deposited.

The sequence will carry on until up to 400 eggs are laid. Spawning can vary from a matter of one hour to two days. One mistake is to remove the parents, thinking that they have completed spawning, when, in fact, they are simply having a much-needed rest.

The Peppered Catfish, in common with other *Corydoras* catfish, will occasionally make a meal of their own eggs. After they have finished breeding, all the fish should be removed from the tank.

EGG AND FRY CARE

The eggs are quite large, about 1.5 mm (^{1}/16 in) in diameter, and take about four days to hatch. Through the opaque eggs, it is possible to see the developing embryos. On hatching, the fry drop to the bottom of the tank and feed for about two days on their yolk-sac. After this, they will need to be supplied food by the fishkeeper.

- **First food**: they will take live brine shrimp nauplii, which can be supplemented with microworm.
- **Second foods**: Peppered Catfish growth is fairly rapid and the youngsters can soon be weaned on to dry foods such as flake, and sinking pellets.

Every week, change about 25 per cent of the tank water, more if the fry has been overfed and if there is a chance of uneaten food being left in the tank.

GROWING ON

Because it is possible to have large broods of these fish, which will grow quickly if fed well, they will need to be moved into larger growing-on tanks.

CHAPTER 11

GOLDEN-EYED CICHLID

This fish, *Nannacara anomala*, is one of many species of cichlids classed as 'dwarf', the males reaching 8 cm (3 in) and the females somewhat smaller at 5 cm (2 in). It is an attractive fish and is often seen in dealers' tanks. It is also easy to breed, making it a good fish for that first-time cichlid breeding project.

TANK SET-UP

Despite their small size, a breeding pair will need a tank with a minimum size of 60 x 30 x 30 cm (24 x 12 x 12 in), to allow the pair to use it as a home and a nursery. On the bottom of the tank put a bed of medium-sized aquarium gravel and two 75 mm (3 in) clay flowerpots placed on their sides for the fish to take cover, if needed. Near the centre of the tank place a flat stone about 75 mm (3 in) in diameter; this is for the female to deposit her eggs.

An adult male *Nannacara anomala* – an ideal candidate for a first-time cichlid breeding project.

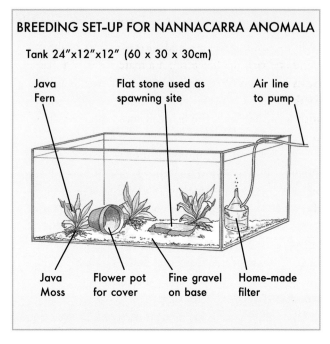

BREEDING SET-UP FOR NANNACARRA ANOMALA

Tank 24"x12"x12" (60 x 30 x 30cm)

Java Fern

Flat stone used as spawning site

Air line to pump

Java Moss

Flower pot for cover

Fine gravel on base

Home-made filter

Nannacara species are classed as open spawners (i.e. they prefer to breed in open areas of tank on flat surfaces, such as stones or rocks). Provide plants such as Java Fern (*Microsorium pteropus*) and Java Moss (*Vesicularia dubyana*) to give extra cover and security for the protection of the parents and fry during breeding.

Filtration is supplied by home-made filters (see page 13) and the temperature set to 25°C (77°F).

WATER CONDITIONS
Suitable water conditions for breeding are pH 6.2 to 7.2 pH, and a hardness of 3 to 6 dH.

BREEDING PROCEDURE
Dwarf cichlids such as *N. anomala* like to choose their own partners, so it is advisable to attain a small group

of fish – say, five to six – and allow them to establish a bond and pair up. Then select a mated pair and place them in the breeding tank. On a varied diet of flake foods, frozen bloodworm, and, if possible, a live food such as whiteworm, the fish will come into breeding condition.

When breeding is imminent, the female will take on a stunning checkerboard pattern. The normal breeding site will be the flat stone and both fish will start to clean the surface of all algae and debris prior to spawning.

Spawning commences with the female laying her adhesive amber-coloured eggs on the stone, with the male fertilising them immediately. More than 100 eggs can be deposited on the stone and the smaller female will take control over the eggs.

The male is not welcome near the egg clutch and will be driven away by the female with some vigour. He will probably take refuge in one of the plant pots; this is where the larger tank comes into its own by giving the male a chance to hide. It is best to remove him at this stage and let the female guard the eggs.

The female will develop a distinctive checked pattern when ready to breed.

On the third day, the female, using her mouth, will gently burst the eggs. The yolk-sac larvae will be seen as a wriggling mass. At this time, she may move them into one of the flowerpots, leaving them only during times when she needs to feed. By the seventh day, the fry will be free-swimming and staying close to their mother *en masse*. To see this amazing sight is a very good reason to breed fish.

GROWING ON

Like many species of dwarf cichlids, the female can get frustrated when guarding her brood as they grow, and will at times eat them.

The fishkeeper must look out for these signs and remove her. The fry are able to survive without their mother after a week of free swimming.

The fry will take brine shrimp nauplii and microworms as first foods. On this diet, they can attain 18 mm ($^3/_4$ in) in length by six weeks old. At this stage, it is best to move them on to a larger tank.

CONCLUSION

When you can breed the egg-laying tropical fish discussed in this book, the same methods can be adapted to breed other similar species of fish. With experience, you may even wish to tackle one of the so-called problem fish, such as the Cardinal Tetra...

Fish breeding opens up a whole new world for the fishkeeper and it is not just confined to someone with the fish house that holds large numbers of tanks. With commonsense and using the methods outlined in this book, you too can become a successful fish breeder.